Volcanoes

By Lucy Floyd

CELEBRATION PRESS
Pearson Learning Group

Contents

Eruption!

In 1883, on an island in Indonesia, a volcano called Krakatoa erupted. It produced one of the largest explosions ever recorded on Earth. The blast was heard almost 3,000 miles away. It covered nearby islands with up to 200 feet of ash. After the eruption was over, only one-third of Krakatoa was left.

Have you ever wondered what causes volcanoes like Krakatoa to explode? In this book, you'll find out. You can also read about what causes volcanoes, how these fiery creations affect people, and how scientists study them.

This picture shows what Krakatoa might have looked like when it erupted in 1883.[1]

The Life of a Volcano

The inside of the Earth is so hot that some of the solid rock melts to form hot, liquid rock called **magma**. A volcano is an opening in the Earth's outer shell, or crust, through which magma flows. The liquid magma also contains gases. Magma slowly rises toward the Earth's surface. It collects in an underground pool called a magma chamber. Magma can build up in a magma chamber for thousands of years.

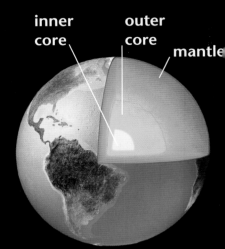

inner core

outer core

mantle

▲ Magma is melted rock that rises to the Earth's surface from the mantle.

Inside a Volcano

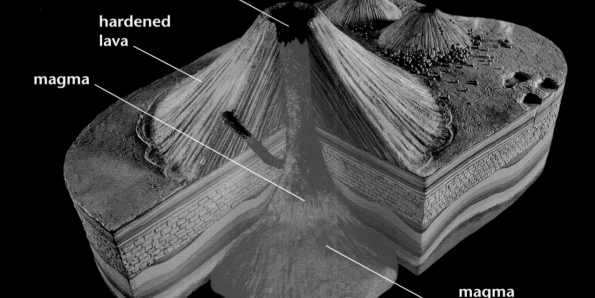

vent

hardened lava

magma

magma chamber

As the chamber fills, the magma presses harder and harder against the solid rock around it. Eventually, magma, gases, and ash push through or blast a hole, called a **vent**, in the Earth's surface and erupt. The eruption may occur on a mountain, on flat land, or under the sea.

Once magma leaves the vent, it is called **lava**. As the hot lava cools, it hardens into rock. This rock can build up for hundreds of years and form a mountain. Sometimes islands are formed in this way.

This lava is flowing from Kilauea volcano, Big Island, Hawaii.▼

A theory called **plate tectonics** explains how volcanoes form. Scientists believe that the Earth's crust is made up of huge sheets of rock called plates. The plates drift or slide slowly over partly melted rock. Volcanoes form at the edges, or boundaries, where two plates meet.

Sometimes the plates bump into each other. One plate may then push under the other. Part of it may melt in the Earth's heat. Other times, the edges of the plates crumple up to form a mountain. In both cases, magma may be released.

Earth's Plates

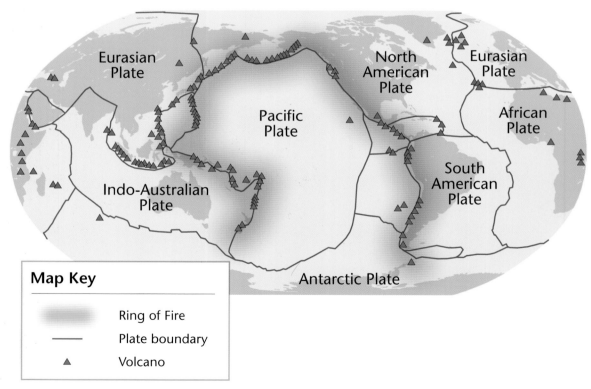

The seven largest plates carry whole continents and oceans.

Many plates bump into each other around the Pacific Ocean in an area called the Ring of Fire. This is one of the largest volcano zones in the world.

Plates can also move apart. This usually happens on the ocean floor. Magma then rises up between the plates. Sometimes this creates underwater mountain ranges.

Not all volcanoes occur near the edges of a plate. A volcano may form above a **hot spot**, which is a source of great heat in the mantle, just below a plate.

The Galápagos Islands are volcanic islands that formed over a hot spot in the Pacific Ocean. ▼

Plate Movements

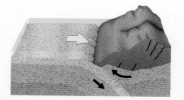

plates colliding

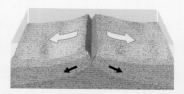

plates moving apart

Volcanoes erupt because pressure forces magma to the surface. How a volcano erupts depends on the amount of water vapor and other gases in the liquid rock. If there is very little gas, the eruption will be quiet. If there is a lot of gas, the eruption will be violent.

It's like the difference between opening a bottle of juice and a bottle of soda. The juice doesn't have much gas in it. There are few bubbles and not much sound when the juice bottle opens. When the soda bottle is opened, there is a lot of sound as the gas trapped in the soda escapes. Sometimes the liquid bubbles out of the bottle.

A Volcanic Eruption

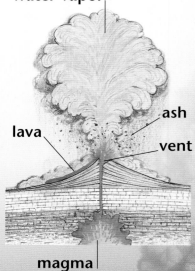

gas, dust, and water vapor

ash

lava

vent

magma

Mount Ruapehu is an active volcano in New Zealand.

Scientists group volcanoes according to how often they erupt. An **active** volcano is one that is erupting or is showing signs that it may erupt soon. A **dormant**, or sleeping, volcano has not erupted for a long time. This kind of volcano may be quiet for thousands of years. However, it may become active again in the future. An **extinct** volcano is one that has not erupted for more than 10,000 years. Scientists do not expect it to erupt ever again.

▲ Mount Garibaldi in Canada last erupted about 10,000 years ago.

▲ This lake in Visoke, Rwanda, has formed in the crater of an extinct volcano.

Volcanic Landforms

Volcanic landforms are found in many places in the world in different shapes and sizes. They help change the surface of the planet. When volcanoes erupt, they send out ash, dust, hot gas, rocks, and lava that change the land features around them.

Some volcanoes form mountains. Other volcanoes look almost flat. The volcano's shape depends on the type of eruption. Explosive eruptions usually form volcanoes with steep sides. Gentle eruptions usually form broad, low volcanoes. How often the volcano erupts, and the buildup of materials around the volcano, also affect the volcano's shape.

The Shishaldin volcano in Alaska is a composite volcano.

▲ This volcanic crater, or **caldera**, is on Lanzarote in the Canary Islands.

Types of Volcanoes

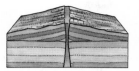

Fissure Volcano

A fissure volcano forms when plates move apart, allowing lava to escape through a crack, or fissure.

Shield Volcano

A shield volcano forms from lava that gently spreads out in all directions.

Dome Volcano

A dome volcano forms when lava blocks the vent, cools, and breaks apart. New lava covers the cool lava, forming a rounded dome.

Ash-Cinder Volcano

An ash-cinder volcano forms when ash and other loose, solid material called cinder, blasts from the vent.

Composite Volcano

A composite volcano forms when lava and ash build up. It is steep near the top and flatter near the bottom.

Caldera Volcano

A caldera is a giant hole. It can form when a magma chamber empties and the volcano collapses.

Rocks and Lava

Volcanoes produce rocks and lava that build up on the Earth's surface. **Igneous rocks** are formed from magma. Fragments of igneous rock may blast out of the vent during an eruption. These pieces are called **tephra** (TEHF-ruh). Some are bigger than baseballs. These large fragments are called bombs.

Tephra also includes smaller fragments. These small fragments are called lapilli, which means "little stones." Ash fragments are smaller than lapilli. Dust fragments are the smallest fragments.

This fast-flowing lava is called pahoehoe lava.

Types of Tephra

bomb

lapilli

ash

dust

The lava that flows out of a volcano is very hot. It may have a temperature of more than 2,000 degrees Fahrenheit. As the lava flows onto the surface, it cools and hardens into different kinds of igneous rock.

Liquid, fast-flowing lava forms smooth folds that look like coils of rope. This unbroken rock is called **pahoehoe** (pah-HOH-ee-HOH-ee). Sticky, slow-moving lava hardens into sharp, jagged rock called **aa** (AH-ah). Sometimes, lava is blown into glasslike strands as thin as a human hair and as long as six feet. They are called Pele's Hair. These names come from the Hawaiian language because of the many volcanoes in Hawaii.

Black Sand

You can find black sand on some beaches, such as in Hawaii and New Zealand. Black sand was created when lava flowed into the ocean and shattered as it met cool water. Over time, the waves smashed the pieces together and broke them apart, creating black sand.

pahoehoe

aa

Pele's Hair

Unusual Lava Formations

Lava has created unusual formations in many places. According to legend, giants built the Giant's Causeway in Northern Ireland as a path across the sea. Scientists, however, say that it is a lava flow that cooled and shrank. The six-sided columns shown in the photograph below are the result.

Devils Tower in Wyoming, United States, is another unusual formation. It was formed when lava hardened inside the vent of an extinct volcano. The volcano's walls wore away over time, leaving the lava behind.

Devils Tower

Giant's Causeway

The Undara Lava Tubes in Queensland, Australia, is the largest system of lava tubes in the world. The tubes were formed 190,000 years ago when a volcano erupted. The lava flowed down the volcano into dry river beds. As the lava met cool air, the outside of the lava began to harden. Meanwhile, the hot lava inside the hard shell kept moving, leaving a hollow tube behind.

There are many more unusual volcanic creations. Lava trees form when lava surrounds a tree. When the lava drains away, the tree shape is left behind.

▲ This picture was taken inside the Undara Lava Tubes in north Queensland, Australia.

Near Mauna Loa, Hawaii, lava has coated a tree and hardened around it. ▶

Underwater Volcanoes

The floor of the ocean is much like that of dry land. There are flat plains, mountain ridges, canyons, and **trenches**. There are also many volcanoes. In fact, there are probably more volcanoes under the ocean than on land.

Underwater volcanoes form the same way as land volcanoes. Magma finds a way up to the seafloor's surface. Lava flows out of the vent during each eruption and is cooled by the seawater. The lava gradually builds up higher and higher. The volcano may eventually rise above the sea's surface to form an island. Mauna Kea (MAH-nah KEY-ah) in Hawaii formed this way.

The Ocean Floor

ridge   volcanic island

▲ Mauna Kea is the tallest mountain in the world if measured from its base on the ocean floor.

Underwater eruptions may be violent. When water enters the volcano's vent, it meets hot magma and creates steam. The boiling, steamy water causes an explosion. The eruption takes place with sometimes hundreds of feet of water pressing down on top of it.

The island of Surtsey, near Iceland, was formed by an underwater volcanic eruption. Two plates in the Atlantic Ocean moved apart, causing the eruption. In 1963, the top of the volcano rose above the surface of the sea and became a new island.

▲ The eruption that created the new island of Surtsey lasted for almost four years.

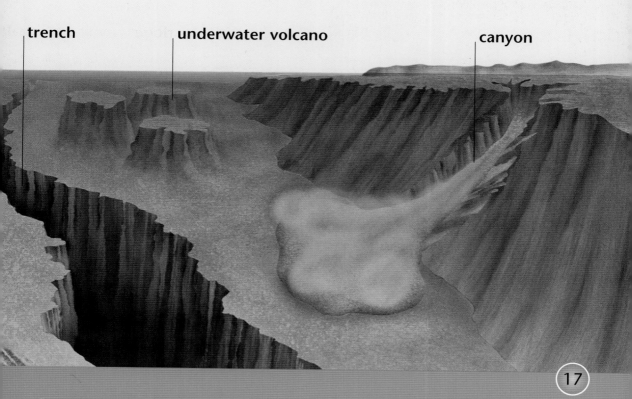

trench   underwater volcano   canyon

Living With Volcanoes

People have lived near volcanoes for thousands of years. For example, Mexico City, Mexico, one of the largest cities in the world, was settled next to a volcano. If volcanoes are so dangerous, why do people live near them?

One reason is that the soil near volcanoes is very fertile. After an eruption, lava and volcanic ash settle into the soil. The **minerals** and chemicals in the lava and ash gradually make the soil fertile so it is good for farming.

More than 1.5 million people live around Mount Vesuvius, a volcano in southern Italy. Olives, nuts, and orange and lemon trees grow well in the area's rich soil. Fertile volcanic soil also helps farmers in El Salvador, Guatemala, and Indonesia.

Farmers plant rice in the fertile soils below Mount Merapi, an active volcano on Java.

Volcanoes also help produce electricity. They heat rocks that are near the Earth's crust. When these rocks heat underground water, it turns to steam. People use this steam to make electricity. This kind of energy is known as **geothermal energy**. Geothermal energy is considered a clean energy source because it does not pollute the air or water.

Countries such as Iceland, New Zealand, and Japan have built plants to collect the steam from geothermal energy resources. Pipes pump water through the naturally hot rock. The steam that is produced is sent through machines that convert it into electricity.

Near a geothermal power plant in Iceland, the naturally heated water is warm enough for swimming. ▼

Even though there are benefits of living near a volcano, it can be risky. Volcanic eruptions have destroyed entire towns and forests. Hot lava is one danger. Ash and toxic gases are also harmful. Ash can block some of the sun's rays, causing global temperatures to fall. It can pollute rivers and kill plants. The gases can also pollute the air and damage the forests. Sometimes, they poison people and animals, too.

Fortunately, there are scientists who study and monitor volcanoes. These **volcanologists** help predict future eruptions and the places that may be at risk. This means that people living near volcanoes can plan what to do in an emergency.

Mount Pinatubo

Entire villages were covered in ash after Mount Pinatubo in the Philippines erupted in 1991. Volcanologists predicted the eruption. Although about 800 people were killed, almost 35,000 people were evacuated and saved because of the early warnings.

◀ Mount St. Helens in the United States destroyed more than 150 square miles of forest when it erupted in 1980.

Volcanologists

Volcanologists study volcanoes in different ways. They study the rocks and ash left by past eruptions to learn about the volcano's history. This helps them predict how the volcano will act in the future.

Volcanologists also study the changes in and around a volcano. They map the volcano's shape and size. They compare this information to earlier maps to see if the volcano is getting bigger. They also use special instruments, called seismometers, to study any ground movement or earthquakes around the volcano. They check the size of cracks in the ground. A change inside and around a volcano can mean that an eruption is likely to occur.

Volcanologists watch from a helicopter as a volcano erupts in Hawaii Volcanoes National Park.

Working near a volcano can be very dangerous. Scientists protect themselves as they gather rocks, gases, and lava to take back to the laboratory. They wear gas masks so that they don't breathe in any poisonous gases. They wear gloves and helmets as they collect hot rocks. They also use a long pole called a hot rod to collect lava from a safe distance.

Studying volcanoes helps us learn what's going on deep inside the planet. Volcanoes have been on Earth longer than people. We can also learn how volcanoes formed and how they might erupt in the future. Learning to predict eruptions will allow us to live more safely with volcanoes.

Robot Volcanologists

Volcanologists have tried to use robots to collect samples from inside volcanoes. The first of these robots, Dante I and II, were too badly damaged to be used again. Scientists do, however, hope to use robots for exploration again in the near future.

Volcanologists wear heat-resistant suits as they gather samples from the hot lava.

Glossary

aa   jagged rock formed from sticky lava

active   a volcano that is erupting or is expected to erupt

caldera   a huge depression, or hole, formed by the collapse of a volcano

dormant   a volcano that is not erupting now, but might again in the future

extinct   a volcano that is not expected to erupt again

geothermal energy   steam from below the Earth's surface that is used to produce heat and electricity

hot spot   extremely hot areas, away from plate edges, where rising magma produces volcanoes

igneous rocks   type of rock formed from melted rock that comes from inside the Earth

lava   magma which has reached the Earth's surface

magma   hot, melted rock deep inside the Earth

minerals   natural substances formed in the Earth that provide nutrients for living things

pahoehoe   smooth, ropy rock formed from runny lava

plate tectonics   the theory stating that the layer just under the Earth's surface is broken into huge pieces, called plates, that float on partly melted rock

tephra   rock fragments that blast out in an eruption

trenches   deep, narrow gaps in the ocean floor caused by the movement of Earth's plates

vent   an opening through which volcanic material erupts

volcanologists   scientists who study volcanoes

Index

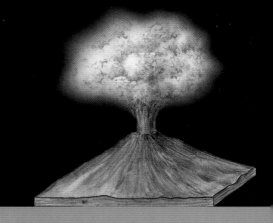